Ha

by Iain Gray

WRITING *to* REMEMBER

Lang**Syne**

PUBLISHING

WRITING *to* REMEMBER

79 Main Street, Newtongrange,
Midlothian EH22 4NA
Tel: 0131 344 0414   Fax: 0845 075 6085
E-mail: info@lang-syne.co.uk
www.langsyneshop.co.uk

Design by Dorothy Meikle
Printed by Printwell Ltd
© Lang Syne Publishers Ltd 2017

ISBN 978-1-85217-468-2

Harrison

MOTTO:
He who conquers endures
(and)
Ready for all things.

CREST:
A serpent
(and)
A demi-lion supporting a chaplet of roses
(and)
A demi-lion rampant holding a laurel branch.

NAME variations include:
Harieson
Harris
Harries
Harryson

Chapter one:

The origins of popular surnames

by George Forbes and Iain Gray

If you don't know where you came from, you won't know where you're going is a frequently quoted observation and one that has a particular resonance today when there has been a marked upsurge in interest in genealogy, with increasing numbers of people curious to trace their family roots.

Main sources for genealogical research include census returns and official records of births, marriages and deaths – and the key to unlocking the detail they contain is obviously a family surname, one that has been 'inherited' and passed from generation to generation.

No matter our station in life, we all have a surname – but it was not until about the middle of the fourteenth century that the practice of being identified by a particular surname became commonly established throughout the British Isles.

Previous to this, it was normal for a person to be identified through the use of only a forename.

But as population gradually increased and there were many more people with the same forename, surnames were adopted to distinguish one person, or community, from another.

Many common English surnames are patronymic in origin, meaning they stem from the forename of one's father – with 'Johnson,' for example, indicating 'son of John.'

It was the Normans, in the wake of their eleventh century conquest of Anglo-Saxon England, a pivotal moment in the nation's history, who first brought surnames into usage – although it was a gradual process.

For the Normans, these were names initially based on the title of their estates, local villages and chateaux in France to distinguish and identify these landholdings.

Such grand descriptions also helped enhance the prestige of these warlords and generally glorify their lofty positions high above the humble serfs slaving away below in the pecking order who had only single names, often with Biblical connotations as in Pierre and Jacques.

The only descriptive distinctions among the peasantry concerned their occupations, like 'Pierre the swineherd' or 'Jacques the ferryman.'

Roots of surnames that came into usage in England not only included Norman-French, but also Old French, Old Norse, Old English, Middle English, German, Latin, Greek, Hebrew and the Gaelic languages of the Celts.

The Normans themselves were originally Vikings, or 'Northmen', who raided, colonised and eventually settled down around the French coastline.

The had sailed up the Seine in their longboats in 900AD under their ferocious leader Rollo and ruled the roost in north eastern France before sailing over to conquer England in 1066 under Duke William of Normandy – better known to posterity as William the Conqueror, or King William I of England.

Granted lands in the newly-conquered England, some of their descendants later acquired territories in Wales, Scotland and Ireland – taking not only their own surnames, but also the practice of adopting a surname, with them.

But it was in England where Norman rule and custom first impacted, particularly in relation to the adoption of surnames.

This is reflected in the famous *Domesday Book*, a massive survey of much of England and Wales, ordered by William I, to determine who owned what, what it was worth and therefore how much they were liable to pay in taxes to the voracious Royal Exchequer.

Completed in 1086 and now held in the National Archives in Kew, London, 'Domesday' was an Old English word meaning 'Day of Judgement.'

This was because, in the words of one contemporary chronicler, "its decisions, like those of the Last Judgement, are unalterable."

It had been a requirement of all those English landholders – from the richest to the poorest – that they identify themselves for the purposes of the survey and for future reference by means of a surname.

This is why the *Domesday Book*, although written in Latin as was the practice for several centuries with both civic and ecclesiastical records, is an invaluable source for the early appearance of a wide range of English surnames.

Several of these names were coined in connection with occupations.

These include Baker and Smith, while Cooks, Chamberlains, Constables and Porters were to be found carrying out duties in large medieval households.

The church's influence can be found in names such as Bishop, Friar and Monk while the popular name of Bennett derives from the late fifth to mid-sixth century Saint Benedict, founder of the Benedictine order of monks.

The early medical profession is represented by Barber, while businessmen produced names that include Merchant and Sellers.

Down at the village watermill, the names that cropped up included Millar/Miller, Walker and Fuller, while other self-explanatory trades included Cooper, Tailor, Mason and Wright.

Even the scenery was utilised as in Moor, Hill, Wood and Forrest – while the hunt and the chase supplied names that include Hunter, Falconer, Fowler and Fox.

Colours are also a source of popular surnames, as in Black, Brown, Gray/Grey, Green and White, and would have denoted the colour of the clothing the person habitually wore or, apart from the obvious exception of 'Green', one's hair colouring or even complexion.

The surname Red developed into Reid, while

Blue was rare and no-one wanted to be associated with yellow.

Rather self-important individuals took surnames that include Goodman and Wiseman, while physical attributes crept into surnames such as Small and Little.

Many families proudly boast the heraldic device known as a Coat of Arms, as featured on our front cover.

The central motif of the Coat of Arms would originally have been what was borne on the shield of a warrior to distinguish himself from others on the battlefield.

Not featured on the Coat of Arms, but highlighted on page three, is the family motto and related crest – with the latter frequently different from the central motif.

Adding further variety to the rich cultural heritage that is represented by surnames is the appearance in recent times in lists of the 100 most common names found in England of ones that include Khan, Patel and Singh – names that have proud roots in the vast sub-continent of India.

Echoes of a far distant past can still be found in our surnames and they can be borne with pride in commemoration of our forebears.

Chapter two:

Saxons and Normans

A name that is almost interchangeable with the equally popular form of 'Harris', 'Harrison' indicates 'son of Harry' – with 'Harry' itself being a diminutive, or pet form, of 'Henry'.

Among the 30 commonest names in both the United Kingdom and the United States, it is also found in a number of other forms that include Harryson and Harries.

It is thought to have been present on British shores for a considerable period of time before the Norman Conquest of 1066, with a further influx of names following Duke William of Normandy's invasion.

This means that bearers of the Harrison name today may be of either original Anglo-Saxon stock or of Norman blood.

Flowing through the veins of many people of English birth today is indeed the blood of those Germanic tribes who invaded and settled in the south and east of the island of Britain from about the early fifth century.

Known as the Anglo-Saxons, they were composed of the Jutes, from the area of the Jutland Peninsula in modern Denmark, the Saxons from Lower Saxony, in modern Germany and the Angles from the Angeln area of Germany.

It was the Angles who gave the name 'Engla land', or 'Aengla land' – better known as 'England.'

They held sway in what became England from approximately 550 to 1066, with the main kingdoms those of Sussex, Wessex, Northumbria, Mercia, Kent, East Anglia and Essex.

Whoever controlled the most powerful of these kingdoms was tacitly recognised as overall 'king' – one of the most noted being Alfred the Great, King of Wessex from 871 to 899.

It was during his reign that the famous *Anglo-Saxon Chronicle* was compiled – an invaluable source of Anglo-Saxon history – while Alfred was designated in early documents as *Rex Anglorum Saxonum*, King of the English Saxons.

Through the Anglo-Saxons, also simply referred to as the Saxons, the language known as Old English developed, later transforming from the eleventh century into Middle English – sources from which many popular English surnames of today, such as Harrison, derive.

By 1066, England had become a nation with several powerful competitors to the throne.

In what were extremely complex family, political and military machinations, the English monarch was Harold II, who had succeeded to the throne following the death of Edward the Confessor.

But his right to the throne was contested by two powerful competitors – his brother-in-law King Harold Hardrada of Norway, in alliance with Tostig, Harold II's brother, and Duke William II of Normandy.

In what has become known as The Year of Three Battles, Hardrada invaded England and gained victory over the Saxon king on September 20th at the battle of Fulford, in Yorkshire.

Five days later, however, Harold II decisively defeated his brother-in-law and brother at the battle of Stamford Bridge.

But Harold had little time to celebrate his victory, having to immediately march south from Yorkshire to encounter a mighty invasion force, led by Duke William of Normandy that had landed at Hastings, in East Sussex.

Harold's battle-hardened but exhausted force of Saxon soldiers confronted the Normans on October 25th in a battle subsequently depicted on the Bayeux tapestry – a 23ft. long strip of embroidered linen thought to have been commissioned eleven years after the event by the Norman Odo of Bayeux.

It was at the top of Senlac Hill that Harold drew up a strong defensive position, building a shield wall to repel Duke William's cavalry and infantry.

The Normans suffered heavy losses, but through a combination of the deadly skill of their archers and the ferocious determination of their cavalry they eventually won the day.

Saxon morale had collapsed on the battle-field as word spread through the ranks that Harold had been killed – the Bayeux Tapestry depicting this as having happened when the English king was struck by an arrow to the head.

Amidst the carnage of the battlefield, it was difficult to identify Harold – the last of the Anglo-Saxon kings.

Some sources assert William ordered his body to be thrown into the sea, while others state it was secretly buried at Waltham Abbey.

What is known with certainty, however, is

that William in celebration of his great victory founded Battle Abbey, near the site of the battle, ordering that the altar be sited on the spot where Harold was believed to have fallen.

William was declared King of England on December 25th, and what followed was the complete subjugation of his Saxon subjects.

Those Normans who had fought on his behalf were rewarded with the lands of Saxons, many of whom sought exile abroad as mercenaries.

Within an astonishingly short space of time, Norman manners, customs and law were imposed on England – laying the basis for what subsequently became established 'English' custom and practice.

In England, the greatest concentration of bearers of the name was in present-day Lancashire – but they figure prominently in the overall history of the nation.

Major General Thomas Harrison, born in 1606 in Newcastle-under-Lyme, was the English Parliamentarian who was one of the signatories in 1649 of the death warrant of Charles I.

King of England, Scotland and Ireland from 1625 until his execution, the headstrong Stuart monarch had incurred the wrath of Parliament by his insistence on the 'divine right' of monarchs.

Added to this was Parliament's fear of Catholic 'subversion' against the state and the king's stubborn refusal to grant demands for religious and constitutional concessions.

Matters came to a head with the outbreak of the English Civil War in 1642, with Parliamentary forces, known as the New Model Army and commanded by Oliver Cromwell and Sir Thomas Fairfax, arrayed against the Royalist army of the king.

In what became an increasingly bloody and complex conflict, spreading to Scotland and Ireland and with rapidly shifting loyalties on both sides, the 49-year-old king was eventually captured and executed on the orders of Parliament.

This was an act for which Major General Thomas Harrison paid dearly following the Restoration of Charles II in 1660.

Found guilty of regicide – the killing of a monarch – he was hanged, drawn and quartered near the site of present-day Charing Cross, London.

Chapter three:

Battle honours

In later centuries and in much different conflicts, bearers of the Harrison name have gained distinction – with no fewer than three being honoured with the Victoria Cross (VC), the highest award for valour in the face of enemy action for British and Commonwealth forces.

Born in 1832 in Castleboro, Co. Wexford, John Harrison was an Irish recipient of the award.

A leading seaman in the Royal Navy during the Indian Mutiny, it was in November of 1857 at Lucknow that he and fellow seaman Nowell Salmon volunteered to go ashore from their vessel and, climbing a tree, the pair fired on an enemy position.

Both men were awarded the VC for their actions, while Harrison died in 1865 as a result of wounds he had received.

His VC is now on display at the National Maritime Museum in Greenwich, London.

Born in 1890 in Kingston upon Hull, East Yorkshire, Jack Harrison was a First World War recipient of both the Military Cross and the VC.

A lieutenant in the East Yorkshire Regiment, 11th Battalion, he was awarded the Military Cross (MC) for his actions on the Western Front in March of 1917 when he led a patrol into no-man's land and captured a German soldier with vital information on enemy dispositions.

A professional rugby player in Hull before the start of the war, he was awarded the VC after he was killed leading an attack on an enemy position in a wood near Oppy, Pas-de-Calais, single-handedly attacking a machine-gun nest.

His VC is now on display in the Prince of Wales's Own Regiment of Yorkshire Museum, York.

On the high seas, Lieutenant-Commander Arthur Harrison was the First World War recipient of the VC born in 1886 in Torquay, Devon.

In common with VC winner Jack Harrison, he had been a rugby player and was capped twice for England before the outbreak of war.

He was posthumously awarded the VC for his actions in April of 1918 during the Zeebrugge Raid – the attempt by the British to block the Zeebrugge-Bruges Canal. In charge of the Royal Navy storming parties on the mission, he led his men on, despite serious wounds, before being killed.

His VC is now on display at the Britannia Royal Naval College, Dartmouth, Devon.

Also during the carnage of the First World War, Edward Harrison, born in 1869, was the British chemical scientist credited with the invention of the first serviceable gas mask, in the form of the large box respirator, used extensively throughout the war.

Head of the Burroughs and Welcome analytical laboratory and also instrumental in the compilation of the *British Pharmaceutical Codex*, he died a year after the war ended in 1918.

The Edward Harrison Memorial Prize of the Royal Society of Chemistry is named in his honour.

Known as "Bomber" Harris, Sir Arthur Harris was the British Air Chief Marshall born in Cheltenham, Gloucestershire, in 1892.

It was as Air Officer Commanding-in-Chief of RAF Bomber Command during the Second World War that, from early in 1943, he was in charge of the devastating and controversial 'area', as opposed to 'precision' bombing of German cities – a policy with which he had been tasked by his political masters.

Raised to the peerage as a Baronet in 1953 at the insistence of Winston Churchill, after having earlier refused the honour, he died in 1984.

The controversy over his bombing strategy continues to this day – with the late Queen Mother being jeered by protestors when she unveiled a statue of Harris outside the RAF Church of St Clement Danes, London, in 1992.

From the battlefield to American politics, a famous dynasty of bearers of the Harrison name was prominent in the nation's political affairs.

The son of a well-established family of Harrisons that had settled in Virginia, Benjamin Harrison V was a leading figure throughout the American War of Independence from 1775 to 1783 against its colonial master Britain.

Born in Charles City County in 1726 and a wealthy planter, he was a Virginia delegate to the Continental Congress of 1774 to 1777 and one of the distinguished signatories to the 1776 Declaration of Independence.

Governor of Virginia from 1781 to 1784, he died in 1791, while Harrison County, West Virginia, is named in his honour.

An ancestor of the Confederate General Robert E. Lee, he was also the father of William Henry Harrison, 9th President of the United States and the great-grandfather of his namesake,

Benjamin Harrison, 23rd President of the United States.

Both a military officer and politician, William Henry Harrison was born in Charles City County in 1773.

Originally coming to public attention as the commander of U.S. forces against Native Americans at the 1811 battle of Tippecanoe, where he earned the nickname "Old Tippecanoe", he later served as a Representative and Senator for Ohio.

Serving as 9th President of the United States from March 4th 1841 until his death exactly a month later, he holds the record of the shortest tenure of office in U.S. Presidential history.

The last president to be born before the Declaration of Independence, he was also the first president to die in office and, until the election of President Ronald Reagan in 1981 at the age of 69, the oldest president when elected.

Harrison in New Jersey and Harrison, Ohio, are named in his honour.

He was a grandfather of Benjamin Harrison, who served from March 4th 1889 to March 4th 1893 as 23rd President of the United States.

Born in 1833 in North Bend, Ohio, he served

as a Brigadier General in the Union Army of the Cumberland during the American Civil War of 1861 to 1865.

A Republican, he served as senator for Ohio before his election as President, and was one of the first American politicians to argue forcibly, although unsuccessfully, for legislation to protect the voting rights for African Americans and for federal funding for education.

He died in 1901, while a Harrison commemorative U.S. Dollar coin was issued in 2012.

Back across the Atlantic to Britain, one particularly inventive eighteenth century bearer of the Harrison name was John Harrison who, as the inventor of the marine chronometer, revolutionised the complex technique of navigation at sea.

Born in 1693 in Foulby, near Wakefield, Yorkshire, the self-trained carpenter later turned his talents to watchmaking.

It was in 1730 that the British Parliament offered a prize of £20,000 – worth approximately £2.87m today – for the invention of a device that could solve the problem of establishing the East-West position, or longitude, of a vessel at sea.

Harrison applied himself to the challenge

and, after many setbacks, it was not until more than 40 years after the prize was first offered that he had invented a marine clock found to be accurate to within one third of one second per day.

Despite the years of effort that had effectively broken his health, Parliament refused to grant him the total prize money.

It was not until an angry King George III intervened on his behalf that Parliament grudgingly awarded him £8,750, with an agreement for further payments in instalments over the years.

But he died only four years later, in 1776, with neither he nor his family ever receiving the full sum of money originally promised.

Meanwhile one indication of the importance of his invention and the dedication with which he applied himself to the work is that in May of 2002 he came 39th in a BBC poll of the 100 Greatest Britons.

Chapter four:

On the world stage

From music and acting to sport and the sciences, bearers of the Harrison and Harris names have stamped their mark at an international level.

Famous not only as a member, along with Paul McCartney, John Lennon and Ringo Starr, of the Beatles, but also as a highly successful solo artist in his own right, **George Harrison** was the guitarist, singer and songwriter born in 1943.

Known as 'the quiet Beatle' and also a devotee of Indian mysticism, he wrote a number of Beatle hits that include *Here Comes the Sun*, *Something* and *While My Guitar Gently Weeps*, while as a solo artist his albums include the 1968 *Wonderwall Music*, the 1970 *All Things Must Pass* and his 1981 *Somewhere in England*.

His 1971 A Concert for Bangladesh, featuring other musicians who included Bob Dylan and Eric Clapton, raised more than $24m for humanitarian efforts in Bangladesh.

The recipient of a number of honours and awards that include induction into the Rock and Roll

Hall of Fame and the first recipient, in 1992, of the Billboard Century Award for music artists with significant bodies of work, he died in 2001.

Married to the actress Pattie Boyd from 1966 to 1974, and then to record company secretary Olivia Arias, his George Harrison Humanitarian Fund for UNICEF continues to contribute to a number of humanitarian efforts across the world.

His son, **Dhani Harrison**, born in 1978 in Windsor, Berkshire, is the musician who helped to complete George Harrison's last album, *Brainwashed*, released a year after his death.

An inductee of the Country Music Hall of Fame and the American Academy of Arts and Sciences, **EmmyLou Harris** is the American singer and songwriter whose best-selling albums include the 2005 *The Connection*.

Born in 1947 in Birmingham, Alabama, she has also performed with musicians who include Willie Nelson, Neil Young and Bob Dylan.

Also in contemporary music, **Jerry Harrison** is the American musician, songwriter and producer best known as a guitarist and keyboardist for the band Talking Heads.

Born in 1949 in Milwaukee, his solo albums

include the 1981 *The Red and the Black* and, from 1990, *Walk on Water*.

A rhythm and blues singer, guitarist, pianist and harmonica player, **Wilbert Harrison** was the American musician born in 1929 in Charlotte, North Carolina, and who died in 1994.

His 1959 hit *Kansas City*, written by Jerry Leiber and Mike Stoller, was given a Grammy Hall of Fame Award in 2001, while it has also been named by the Rock and Roll Hall of Fame as one of 500 songs that shaped the genre.

Bearers of the Harrison and Harris names have also made their name in the world of stage and film.

An actor of both stage and screen, **Sir Rex Harrison** was born Reginald Carey Harrison in 1908 in Huyton, Lancashire.

Serving as a Flight Lieutenant in the RAF during the Second World War, he had earlier made his film debut in the 1930 *The Great Game*.

Known for his role in the 1964 *My Fair Lady*, for which he won an Academy Award for Best Actor, his other major screen credits include the 1967 *Dr Doolittle*, from which the song *Talk to the Animals* won an Academy Award for Best Original Song.

He died in 1990, two years after being knighted in recognition of his services to acting.

He was the father of the actor, singer and British competitive skier **Noel Harrison**, born in London in 1934 and who died in 2013.

Representing Britain as a skier in both the 1952 and 1956 Winter Olympics, he was also known for his 1968 hit single *The Windmills of Your Mind*, the theme tune for the film *The Thomas Crown Affair*, and winner of an Academy award for Best Original Song.

Winner of a 1963 Academy Award nomination for Best Actor in a Leading Role for *This Sporting Life* and the same in 1970 for *The Field*, **Richard Harris** was the Irish actor, theatrical producer, director and writer born in 1930 in Limerick.

His film debut was the 1958 *Alive and Kicking*, while his other notable film credits include *Camelot*, from 1967, the 1970 *Cromwell* and, before his death in 2002, the role of Albus Dumbledore in the first two films of the *Harry Potter* series.

Also on the screen, **Bret Harrison**, born in 1982 in Portland, Oregon, is the American actor and singer best known for his roles in U.S. television series that include *The Loop*, *Breaking In*, *Grounded for Life* and *Reaper*.

Best known for her role from 1980 to 1982 as Cindy Snow on the hit U.S. sitcom *Three's Company*, **Jenilee Harrison** is the actress born in 1959 in Los Angeles.

From 1984 to 1986 she played the role of Jamie Ewing in *Dallas*, while her film credits include the 1984 *Tanks*.

Married for a time to the American film producer Richard D. Zanuck, **Linda Harrison**, born in 1945 in Maryland, is the actress whose film roles include that of Nova in the 1968 *Planet of the Apes*.

Bearers of the Harrison name have also excelled, and continue to excel, in the highly competitive world of sport.

Born in 1965 in Milwaukee, Wisconsin, **Kenny Harrison** is the American former track and field athlete who won the gold medal in the triple jump event at the 1991 World Championships in Tokyo and in the same event five years later at the Olympics in Atlanta.

Also in athletics, **Alvin Harrison**, born in 1974 in Orlando, Florida, along with his twin brother

Calvin Harrison, made Olympic history in 2000 by becoming the first twins ever to compete in and win Olympic gold medals on the same relay team.

In the boxing ring, **Scott Harrison**, born in 1977 in Bellshill, Lanarkshire is the Scottish boxer, nicknamed "The Real McCoy", who has held the title of World Boxing Organisation (WBO) featherweight champion.

Also in the ring, **Audley Harrison**, nick-named "A-Force", is the heavyweight boxer born in London in 1971 and who turned professional in 2001.

The first British boxer to win, in 2000, an Olympic gold medal in the super heavyweight division, he was awarded an MBE in the same year.

On the cricket pitch, **Jim Harrison**, born in 1941 in Lurgan, Co. Armagh, is the Irish former cricketer who played for the Ireland cricket team between 1969 and 1977.

In the Canadian national sport of ice hockey, **James Harrison** is the former professional player who played more than 300 games in the National Hockey League and more than 230 in the World Hockey Association.

Born in 1947 in Bonnyville, Alberta, he played for teams that include the Boston Bruins,

Toronto Maple Leafs, Edmonton Oilers and Chicago Black Hawks.

From sport to the written word, **Harry Harrison** is the American science fiction author who was born Henry Maxwell Dempsey in Stamford, Connecticut, in 1925.

Main writer during the 1950s and 60s of the *Flash Gordon* newspaper strip, his 1966 novel *Make Room! Make Room!* formed the basis of the 1973 film *Soylent Green*.

Also in the science fiction genre, **Michael Harrison**, born in 1945 in Rugby, Warwickshire, is the British author known for his *Viriconium* series of novels and short stories.

In the sciences, James Merrit Harrison, better known as **James M. Harrison**, was the Canadian scientist who served as director of the Geological Survey of Canada from 1956 to 1964.

Born in 1915 in Regina, Saskatchewan, he also served as president of the International Council of Science from 1966 to 1968; made a Companion of the Order of Canada in 1971, he died in 1990.

Not only a newspaper publisher but also a pioneer of refrigeration techniques, **James Harrison** was born in 1816 near Renton, Dunbartonshire.

Immigrating to Australia from his native Scotland in 1837 after serving an apprenticeship as a printer, he worked for a time in this trade in Sydney before moving to Melbourne.

It was here that he launched the weekly *Geelong Advertiser* – and it was while observing the printing process that he chanced upon something that was destined to revolutionise refrigeration techniques.

He had noticed that when moveable metal type was cleaned with a solution of ether, the evaporating fluid would leave the type cold to the touch.

Applying this, he developed the world's first ice-making machine in 1854, followed only a year later with a patent for the first ever mechanical refrigerator, using an ether vapour compression system.

He died in 1893, while the James Harrison Bridge across the Barwon River in Geelong is named in his honour.

One bearer of the Harrison name who has had a profound effect on the lives of many thousands of children worldwide is the Australian blood donor **James Harrison**.

Born in 1936 and known as "The Man with the Golden Arm", when he first donated blood at the age of 18, it was noticed it contains an extremely rare antibody that prevents infants who receive it from dying of the form of anaemia known as Rhesus Disease.

His blood is given in the form of the special Anti-D Vaccine – developed specifically from his blood.

So precious is this blood that his own life has been insured for $1m, while in May of 2011 he recorded his 1,000th blood donation.

It is in recognition of his role in saving the lives of so many babies that he is honoured as a recipient of the Order of Australia.